A G
and
Fluffy Feathers

Whose little baby are you?

A Grassland Chick

A little chick lives on a hot **grassland**.

grassland

The chick has a long neck and fluffy feathers.

chick

feathers

Who does this little baby belong to?

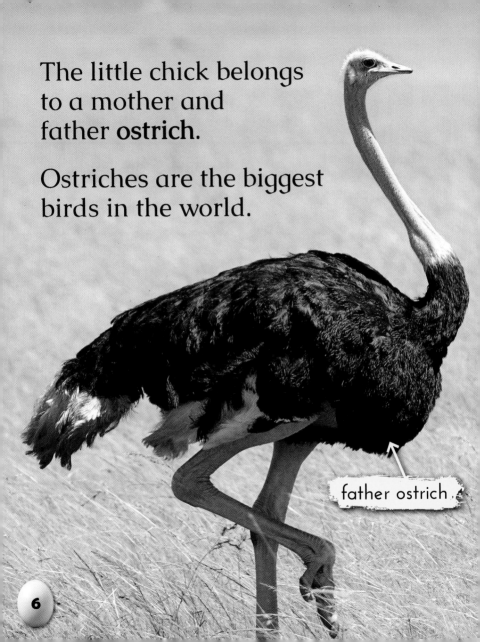

The little chick belongs to a mother and father **ostrich**.

Ostriches are the biggest birds in the world.

father ostrich

mother ostrich

One day, the father ostrich dug a nest hole in the ground.

He dug the hole with his big feet.

The mother ostrich laid seven eggs in the nest.

mother ostrich

eggs

Some other ostriches laid their eggs in the nest, too.

ostrich eggs

Soon, the mother and father ostrich had 21 eggs to care for!

mother ostrich

They took it in turn to sit on the eggs.

father ostrich

The eggs are under here!

11

After 42 days, the chick was ready to **hatch**.

He pecked at the eggshell with his beak.

ostrich chick

beak

eggshell

He pushed at the eggshell
with his feet.

foot

Out he pops!

Now the chick can walk and run.

The other chicks have hatched
from their eggs, too.

chick

The mother and father ostrich look out for lions.

If a lion comes near, the father ostrich chases it away.

lion

15

The mother and father ostrich eat grass, leaves and flowers.

The chick eats grass, too.

one-week-old chick

The ostrich chicks grow
bigger and taller.

When they are six months old, they can run very fast.

six-month-old ostriches

adult male

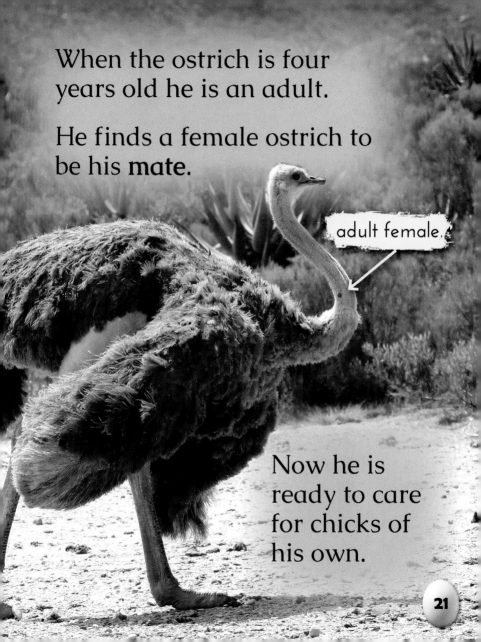

When the ostrich is four years old he is an adult.

He finds a female ostrich to be his **mate**.

adult female

Now he is ready to care for chicks of his own.

Glossary

grassland
A place where the land is covered with grass and other small plants. Only a few trees grow on a grassland.

hatch
To break out of an egg.

mate

An animal's partner with which it has babies.

ostrich

A large bird that is taller than an adult human. Ostriches cannot fly but they are very fast runners.

Ostrich Quiz

1. How many eggs did the parent ostriches care for?

2. How did the ostrich chick break out of his egg?

3. What happens if a lion comes close to the ostrich family?

4. What do ostriches eat?

5. Which picture in the book do you like best? Why?